S0-DPF-123

The Collector's Series / Volume 33

The Junior Chef

by Rena Neff
with Karen Perrino

Dedication

This book is dedicated to my children and grandchildren. May they spend happy hours in their kitchens sharing food, love and laughter.

Acknowledgements

—Cover photograph by Burwell and Burwell
—Cover and page design by Jim Haynes, Graphics Plus, Silver Spring, MD
—Illustrations by Joe Azar, Arlington, VA
—Typesetting by JDL Composition, Baltimore, MD
—Recipe testing by Ben Pierce and Danny Phistry

On the cover: Alexandra Baker and Joshua Crossney prepare Oriental Chicken Salad.

Copyright 1992 by Rena Neff
Printed in U.S.A.
All Rights Reserved

ISBN 0-942320-41-7

The American Cooking Guild
6-A East Cedar Avenue
Gaithersburg, MD 20877
(301) 963-0698

Table of Contents

Family Favorites

Delicious Desserts

A Word to the Cook

Welcome to the world of good eating and good times! Everyone has to eat, so cooking is an important skill. You can prepare food for yourself, family, or friends in your own kitchen which not only tastes delicious but provides energy for your other activities.

Before cooking, talk over your plans with an adult who can show you how to use appliances and help you with some basic cooking techniques as you begin this new adventure.

Never cook alone until given permission. Some kitchen equipment is dangerous if not used properly. You will be allowed to cook more often if you show that you understand and follow safety rules in the kitchen. It also helps if you always leave the kitchen clean.

The next few pages tell about equipment and safety rules. Read them carefully.

A Word to the Adult

As the girl or boy in your home begins to take an interest in "real" cooking, give encouragement and guidance. Cooking is a practical skill and can help your child develop self confidence and self esteem. Encouragement may take the form of setting aside a special place for your novice cook's tools. If so, see the equipment list for suggestions for appropriate tools. You may prefer to have your new cook use family tools and then replace them where they are usually kept. If family tools are used, make sure to give clear guidelines as to which tools may be used and which are off limits until further notice.

Please take a few minutes to go over the next few "getting started" pages with your child, which will give the two of you a chance to discuss equipment and review safety rules. Once guidelines are established, be available as a consultant when your youngster is cooking, but don't jump in and take over the job.

While recipes in this book are meant to be simple enough to be done safely alone, you may want to have your junior chef show you the recipe she or he plans to cook so that you can look for possible trouble spots. Example: You may want to make draining pasta a two-person job. You may also want to look through the book and put a check mark beside recipes you think the child can handle now and save some of the more advanced recipes until your cook has more experience.

We know that you and your child will be proud as skills in the kitchen are developed and some delicious meals are shared with enjoyment.

A Guide to Equipment

Cutting board

Liquid measuring cup

Cookie cutters

Measuring spoons

Hot pads

Rubber spatula

Hand grater

Sandwich spreader

Kitchen scissors

Shaker jar

Knives

Vegetable peeler

Long handled fork

Wooden spoon

Dry measuring cups

Whisk

Other equipment you may need: can opener, pots, pans, cookie sheets, muffin tins and mixing bowls.

Get It Right

A recipe is like a scientific formula. You must use the right ingredients and measure each item correctly. Too much or too little of an ingredient can make the difference between a successful recipe and a dud. Here are some hints on measuring:

Liquid Ingredients should be measured in a clear measuring cup with markings on the side. Pour the ingredient into the measuring cup. Stoop down to counter level or raise the cup to eye level to double-check that the liquid exactly hits the mark. Remove or add more of the ingredient to get it right. When measuring sticky liquids such as honey or corn syrup, make sure to scrape every bit out of the cup and into your mixing bowl.

Dry Ingredients should be measured using measuring spoons or measuring cups of the correct size. Fill the measuring cup. Using a knife or a flat-edged spreader, level off the top, scraping any excess out of the spoon or cup.

The easiest way to measure butter is to use the measuring marks on the side of the wrapper. One stick of butter equals 8 tablespoons or 1/2 cup. A half stick of butter equals 4 tablespoons or 1/4 cup.

To measure brown sugar, spoon the sugar into the measuring cup and pack it down.

To measure flour, scoop it or pour it into the cup and level it off. Use a light touch and do not pack it down.

Basic Cooking Techniques

Here are a few basic cooking techniques:

Beat: use strong, vigorous movements with a fork, spoon, whisk or mixer to make a smooth mixture.

Blend: use a fork, spoon, whisk or mixer to combine two or more ingredients.

Boil: heat a liquid until bubbles appear on the surface.

Chop: cut into pieces of uniform size.

Combine: another word for blend.

Dice: cut into very small pieces of uniform size.

Fold: gently stir two or more ingredients using a fork, spoon, whisk or mixer.

Mince: cut into the smallest possible pieces of uniform size.

Mix: combine two or more ingredients until smooth.

Pare or peel: remove the skin of a food such as an apple or a potato, using small strokes with a vegetable peeler or a paring knife.

Simmer: cook over low heat.

Slice: cut something into slices of uniform thickness.

Whisk: use a strong circular movement of the wrist to beat one or more ingredients.

Safety Tips

1. Always have clean hands and clean utensils. Clean food is healthy food. Dirty food can cause disease. Wear an apron to protect your clothes.

2. Ask which kitchen tools you are allowed to use and make sure you understand how to use each one.

3. Ask an adult to be on hand if you plan to cook something which requires the use of equipment you are not allowed to use alone.

4. Use hot pads to handle hot things. Anything from the oven, stove top, or microwave will be hot.

5. Use large mixing bowls and you will have fewer spills.

6. Wipe up spills with a sponge or damp paper towel as soon as they happen. That way you'll avoid slips or falls and will find clean-up easier.

7. Never hold food in your hands to slice or chop. Always use a cutting board.

8. Use only microwave-safe dishes or paper plates in your microwave. If you're not sure, ask. Let microwaved food cool for a few minutes before eating. Power varies from one microwave to another, so cooking times are approximate.

9. If you see a spark or fire in the microwave, push the stop or clear button. Call for help.

About This Book

The recipes in this book require a minimum of ingredients and cooking time. On the left side of each recipe, you will find the skill level, prep time, cook time and equipment needed.

Recipes marked **Beginner** require only a few ingredients and often require no cooking. Limited skills and time are needed to prepare these recipes.

Recipes marked **Intermediate** call for more ingredients and require more advanced skills such as measuring, beating or chopping. They may require using the stove, oven or microwave.

Recipes marked **Advanced** are designed for the more competent cook who is familiar with most kitchen skills. Advanced recipes may require several steps, more ingredients, and longer preparation time.

Ready: Wash your hands and put on an apron. (An old shirt turned backward with the sleeves cut off will do.) Read the recipe to see what equipment and ingredients you need. Each recipe will list equipment, ingredients, directions and time needed. Gather your equipment and ingredients now.

Set: Read through your ingredient list. Measure and set ingredients on the counter in order of use in the recipe. Read all directions.

Cook: Following directions in the recipe, combine ingredients. Go step by step. Complete each step before going to the next one. When you are finished, make sure everything you have used is washed, dried and put away. Wipe off kitchen counters or other work spaces. Leave everything clean and neat so you will be allowed to cook often.

Thirst Quenchers

Beverages go far beyond drinking a glass of water when you are thirsty or grabbing a glass of milk to wash down a meal. Beverages can soothe you, cool you when you are hot, or warm you when you're not. A beverage can be many things to many people. If you drink an Orange Juicy for breakfast, it is a meal. If you share a milkshake with someone after school, it is an act of friendship. If you sip a cup of punch at a party, it is a refreshment. These beverage recipes are delicious, but they're also quick and easy to mix. Be creative—the only limit is your imagination.

Orange Juicy

Skill Level
beginner

Prep Time
5 minutes

Cook Time
none

Equipment
measuring cup
spoon
blender
serving glass

Here is a quick and easy drink. How could anything so simple to make taste so delicious? Why ask? Just enjoy.

1 cup orange juice
1/2 cup vanilla frozen yogurt

Combine juice and yogurt in blender. Blend until smooth. For a thicker shake, double the amount of frozen yogurt.

Yield: 1 serving

Monkey Shine Shake

Skill Level
beginner

Prep Time
5 minutes

Cook Time
none

Equipment
knife
measuring cup
fork
blender
serving glasses

Monkeys take a shine to bananas and bananas make a great shake. Vary the taste by using a different flavor of frozen yogurt.

1 ripe banana
1 cup milk
1/2 cup vanilla frozen yogurt

Peel bananas and cut into small chunks. Place banana, milk and frozen yogurt in a blender. Cover and blend for 1 minute, or until smooth. Pour into glasses and serve.

Yield: 2 servings

Grandma's Plain Shakes

Skill Level
beginner

Prep Time
5 minutes

Cook Time
none

Equipment
*measuring
  spoons
measuring cup
shaker jar
serving glass*

These two classics are just like the ones Grandma used to make during the "Great Depression." Remember, there was no freezer and usually no refrigerator. These shakes are simple, but refreshing.

Plain Vanilla Shake
*1 teaspoon vanilla extract
2/3 cup milk
1 teaspoon sugar
2 Tablespoons crushed ice*

Put the ingredients into a shaker container or a wide-mouth jar with a lid—Grandma didn't have a blender. Then start to shake and shake . . . the jar of course! Pour into a glass.

Plain Chocolate Shake
*2 1/2 Tablespoons chocolate syrup
2/3 cup milk
2 Tablespoons crushed ice*

Put all ingredients into a jar and shake until well mixed.

Yield: 1 serving

I Scream Shake

Skill Level
beginner

Prep Time
5 minutes

Cook Time
none

Equipment
measuring cup
ice cream scoop
blender
serving glasses

This shake takes its name from the old saying "I scream, you scream, we all scream for ice cream." Vary the flavor according to what kind of ice cream you like or have on hand.

3/4 cup milk
2 cups ice cream

Pour the milk and one cup of the ice cream into a blender. Blend one minute. Add second cup of ice cream. Blend until smooth.

Variations: Add two tablespoons of peanut butter, a chopped banana, *or* two tablespoons of malted milk powder when you add the second cup of ice cream. The "or" means try one of these ideas at a time.

Yield: 2 servings

Sunny Citrus Ades

Skill Level
beginner

Prep Time
6 minutes

Cook Time
none

Equipment
pitcher
measuring cup
cutting board
knife
stirring spoon
serving glasses

Sitting under a shade tree on a summer day, could any thing be more delicious than sipping a citrus ade? Ades are made of citrus juice, water, and sugar served over ice. Start with a pitcher of lemonade for six, then learn to make single glasses of other refreshing ades.

Lemonade
2/3 cup granulated or confectioners sugar
5 cups water
1 cup lemon juice

Put sugar into a pitcher. Add 2 cups water and stir until dissolved. Add remaining water and lemon juice. Stir to mix. Serve in glasses over ice.

Yield: 6 servings

Lemonade for One: Into a large glass, squeeze the juice of half a lemon. Add 3/4 cup water, and 1 to 2 teaspoons sugar. Stir and add ice cubes.

Limeade for One: Into a large glass, squeeze the juice of half of a lime. Add 3/4 cup water, and 1 to 2 teaspoons of sugar. Stir and add ice cubes.

Orangeade for One: Into a large glass, squeeze the juice of one orange. Add 3/4 cup water, and 1 to 2 teaspoons sugar. Stir and add ice cubes.

Fizzy Citrus Ade: To make a fizzy drink, substitute club soda or seltzer water for plain water. Add a marachino cherry, if desired.

Hot Mulled Cider

Skill Level
intermediate

Prep Time
10 minutes

Cook Time
3–6 minutes

Equipment
*measuring cup
sauce pan
four mugs*

For those winter afternoons when you and your friends feel like drinking something warm and soothing, try this.

*4 cups apple cider
3 cloves
1 stick of cinnamon*

Combine all ingredients in a medium saucepan. Warm over medium heat for 3–6 minutes, or until you can smell the spices. Do not boil. To serve, use a ladle to carefully fill each mug. Garnish each serving with a cinnamon stick or a thin slice of lemon.

Yield: 4 servings

Hot Cocoa Mix

Skill Level
beginner

Prep Time
15 minutes

Cook Time
1–2 minutes

Equipment
*mixing bowl
measuring cups
wooden spoon
storage jar*

When you get a yen for a hot cup of cocoa what could be more convenient than to have a jar of your very own cocoa mix on the shelf?

*2 1/2 cups non fat dry milk powder
1 cup confectioner's sugar
1/2 cup unsweetened cocoa powder
marshmallows for garnish, optional*

Combine all ingredients in a large mixing bowl, stirring until well mixed. Store in an air-tight jar or canister with a lid. To make one serving, heat 2/3 cup water in microwave for 1–2 minutes, or until hot. Add 1/3 cup of mix and stir. Garnish with marshmallows if desired.

Yield: 4 cups of mix, 12 servings

For the School Lunch Bunch

What's the best time at school? Many students would say lunch time. Why? Because it's a time to enjoy good food and talk with good friends— a winning combination. Lunch time will be even more special if you take the time to pack lunches so good that they're guaranteed to be "no trade".

Since sandwiches are the centerpiece of bag lunches, recipes are given for a variety of sandwiches. A list of breads, spreads and fillings to mix and match will spark your imagination.

Hero Sandwich

Skill Level
beginner

Prep Time
10 minutes

Cook Time
none

Equipment
sandwich
*   spreader*
paring knife
cutting board

This popular sandwich has many names and variations. It is sometimes called a hero, submarine, Italian sub, or poor boy. Fillings and breads change according to what is available locally. Always it is a sandwich with a variety of fresh fillings on good bread.

1 small French loaf, sandwich roll, hot dog roll
or hamburger bun (your choice)
1 teaspoon mustard
1 Tablespoon mayonnaise
1 slice salami
1 slice ham or bologna
1 slice cheese, any type
1/2 cup shredded lettuce
2 slices tomato, optional
1 slice onion
3 slices of dill pickle

Slice bun if necessary. Put mustard on one side and mayonnaise on the other. Cut meat and cheese slices in half. Layer salami on the mustard side of the bun. Top with the ham or bologna, then the cheese. Continue to layer the sandwich with lettuce, tomato, onion and pickle. Top with second slice of bread. Cut and serve.

Yield: 1 sandwich

COOK'S CORNER
Personalize your lunch bag with markers or a name stamp. Try cutting your sandwiches into mini triangles or squares, or trim off the crusts and cut into thirds for "fingers."

Peanutty Apple Italian Delight

Skill Level
beginner

Prep Time
15 minutes

Cook Time
none

Equipment
*measuring cup
measuring
  spoons
wooden spoon
mixing bowl
hand grater
sandwich
  spreader*

Mama mia! This delicious spread makes a fantastic sandwich, but it also makes a nutritious breakfast or an after school snack.

*1/4 cup ricotta cheese or cottage cheese
3 Tablespoons creamy peanut butter
1/4 teaspoon lemon juice
1/2 teaspoon vanilla extract
1/4 teaspoon ground cinnamon
1 small apple, washed and grated or diced
2 rice cakes or two slices bread, any type*

In a medium mixing bowl, combine ricotta cheese, peanut butter, lemon juice, vanilla extract and cinnamon. Stir until smooth. Add apple and stir to mix. Spread on rice cakes or between two slices of bread.

Yield: 2 open faced or one closed sandwich

Banana Peanut Butter Sandwich

Skill Level
beginner

Prep Time
5 minutes

Cook Time
none

Equipment
*sandwich
  spreader
table knife
measuring
  spoon*

This simple Southern style sandwich can't be beat. It is easy to make and delicious to eat.

*2 slices white or whole wheat bread
2 Tablespoons peanut butter
1 small banana, thinly sliced
1 teaspoon mayonnaise*

Spread one slice of bread with peanut butter. Top with banana slices. Spread mayonnaise on second slice of bread. Close the sandwich. Cut in half.

Yield: 1 sandwich

Tasty Tuna Sandwich

Skill Level
intermediate

Prep Time
15 minutes

Cook Time
none

Equipment
*can opener
mixing bowl
knife
cutting board
measuring cups
measuring
    spoons*

Almost everyone likes a tuna salad sandwich. There are many ways to vary it, but first learn to make it. Later, add your own touches.

*1 6 1/2 oz. can of tuna packed in water
1/4 cup diced celery
1 Tablespoon chopped onion
2 Tablespoons mayonnaise
1 Tablespoon pickle relish or chopped pickle
4 slices bread, any type
lettuce leaf, optional
tomato slices, optional*

Open the can of tuna, drain off the liquid and place in a medium mixing bowl. Using a fork, break tuna chunks into small pieces. Add diced celery, chopped onion, mayonnaise and pickle relish. If the mixture is too dry, add a bit more mayonnaise.

Spread one slice of bread with tuna salad. Add lettuce leaf and sliced tomato, if desired. Top with other slice of bread.

Yield: 2 sandwiches

COOK'S CORNER
To add a special touch to the tuna salad add green grapes and nuts; cubes of avocado, diced pimento and black olives; or grated carrot and chopped hard-boiled eggs.

Egg Salad Sandwich

Skill Level
intermediate

Prep Time
15 minutes

Cook Time
20 minutes

Equipment
small saucepan
cutting board
knife
hot pads
medium bowl

Egg salad is a lunch favorite that is not hard to make. After you master basic egg salad, try adding black or green olives, pimento or deviled ham.

2 hard-boiled eggs, peeled
1 rib celery, diced
1 Tablespoon pickle relish
2 Tablespoons mayonnaise, or to taste
   salt and pepper, to taste

Coarsely chop the peeled, hard-boiled eggs and place in medium mixing bowl. Add celery, pickle relish and two tablespoons of mayonnaise. Stir. If the mixture seems stiff, add more mayonnaise.

To make a sandwich, spread the egg salad on your favorite bread and top with a second slice of bread. Cut and serve.

Yield: 2 sandwiches

COOK'S CORNER
To boil eggs, put two eggs in a pan. Cover with cold water to 1 inch above the eggs. Place on burner over medium-high heat. When the water begins to boil, cover the pot and turn off the stove. Let sit for 15 minutes. Pour hot water off the eggs, and add cold water. When cool enough to handle, crack the shells and peel.

Cream Cheese Tortilla Rolls with Peanut Butter and Jelly

Skill Level
beginner

Prep Time
10 minutes

Cook Time
none

Equipment
*measuring cup
measuring
    spoon
mixing bowl
paper towels
sandwich
    spreader
plastic wrap*

There are two ways to enjoy this tortilla roll—as is, or cut into bite sized rounds. Either way, this unusual sandwich will have you saying, *Ole!* Other things taste good rolled in a tortilla, too. Try it with tuna salad.

*1/4 cup cream cheese
2 Tablespoons jelly or jam (try apricot or
    orange marmalade)
2 Tablespoons crunchy or smooth peanut butter
2 six-inch flour tortillas*

Combine cream cheese with jelly and peanut butter. Stir until smooth.

Warm tortilla in paper towels in the microwave oven for 12 seconds to soften. Spread half the mixture on each tortilla. Roll up tortillas into a log shape. Wrap each in clear plastic wrap. Chill. To serve, slice into 1-inch bite sized rounds or eat whole.

Yield: 2 servings

Personal Favorites

Combine any bread with a spread or filling to create your own favorite lunchtime combination.

Breads
bagel
banana nut
croissant
English muffin
French bread or roll
hamburger bun
hard roll
Italian bread or roll
pita (6″ or mini)
pumpernickel
raisin
rye
Swedish crisp bread
white
whole wheat

Other Things to Fill or Spread
apple slices
baked potato skins
bread sticks
celery stalks
crackers
graham crackers
lettuce leaves
matzo crackers
rice cakes
snow peas
tortillas

Sandwich Makings
any sliced cheese
any sliced or diced fruit
any sliced meat

Peanut Butter Mixtures
Combine peanut butter with:
chopped apple
grated cheese
chopped figs
honey
pineapple
chopped nuts

Cream Cheese Mixtures
Combine cream cheese with:
chopped bacon
grated cheese
chives
chopped fruit
jam or jelly
chopped nuts
sliced olives
pineapple
pickle relish
peanut butter

Salad Mixtures
Follow tuna salad recipe on page 21 but substitute 3/4 cup of any of the following:
shredded cheese
diced chicken
chopped ham
canned salmon
chopped shrimp

After School Snack Attacks

This section is dedicated to those students who arrive home after school and head straight for the kitchen. When you are tired, hungry and thirsty do you eat the first thing in sight? We know a few people who do and they barely taste their food. Why do that when, with a little effort, you can have a really super snack? Here are recipes to stir your imagination and digestive juices beyond the old peanut butter and jelly sandwich with a glass of milk routine. Look these recipes over, then get cooking. The extra few minutes you spend preparing a terrific snack will be time well spent!

Marshmallow Grahamwiches

Skill Level
beginner

Prep Time
5 minutes

Cook Time
1 minute

Equipment
microwave dish

These creamy sandwiches taste like those mouthwatering s'mores that campers like to make over an open fire.

4 graham crackers
24 mini-marshmallows
1/4 cup semi-sweet chocolate chip morsels

Place two graham crackers on a microwave-safe dish. Arrange six mini-marshmallows on the top of each cracker. Top each cracker with a generous sprinkling of chocolate chips and another graham cracker.

Microwave on high for 1 minute. Using a hot pad, remove dish from microwave. Allow to cool slightly and serve.

Yield: 2 cracker sandwiches

Ants On a Log

Skill Level
beginner

Prep Time
10 minutes

Cook Time
none

Equipment
knife
cutting board
butter knife

This traditional snack gets its name because the raisins look like little ants sitting on a celery log.

2 stalks celery
4 Tablespoons smooth peanut butter
2 Tablespoons raisins

Wash celery, trim off top and bottom ends. Using a sandwich spreader or a butter knife, spread the peanut butter into the hollow of each celery piece. Cut each stuffed stalk into three sections. Push raisins into the peanut butter in a design that reminds you of ants on a log.

Yield: 2 servings

No Nonsense Nachos

Skill Level
beginner

Prep Time
10 minutes

Cook Time
1–2 minutes

Equipment
*microwave dish
cheese grater
paring knife
cutting board*

Nachos are a delicious snack that can be varied to suit your individual taste and the ingredients you have in the refrigerator. They are delicious with Cheddar or Monterey Jack cheese, but you can also use mozzarella or processed cheese.

*20 plain tortilla chips
1 cup shredded Cheddar cheese
1/4 cup chopped green onion
2 chopped jalapeno peppers
2 Tablespoons bacon bits*

Garnish:
*chunky salsa
sour cream*

Arrange tortilla chips in a single layer on a large microwave-safe plate. Sprinkle with shredded Cheddar cheese. Top with chopped onions, peppers or bacon bits, to taste.

Microwave on high power for 1 minute. If cheese has not completely melted, continue microwaving for 30 seconds at a time, until cheese melts. Using a hot pad, remove dish from microwave. Garnish the nachos with salsa and sour cream to taste. Serve at once.

Variation: Assemble nachos on a baking sheet and bake in a regular oven at 350° for 3–5 minutes, or until cheese melts.

Yield: 2 servings

Ham 'n Cheese Delights

Skill Level
intermediate

Prep Time
10 minutes

Cook Time
11–13 minutes

Equipment
table knife
cookie sheet
cheese grater
spatula
hot pad
cutting board

The terrific combination of ham and cheese will keep you reaching for "just one more."

1 4-ounce package refrigerator crescent rolls
2 Tablespoons yellow or dijon mustard
1 2-1/4 ounce can deviled ham spread
1/4 cup shredded Cheddar cheese

Preheat oven to 375°. Open the can of rolls and unroll dough. Separate dough into four triangles.

Spread mustard on each piece of dough, top with a spoonful of deviled ham and top with Cheddar cheese. Roll loosely from shortest side of triangle to opposite point. Pat edge of dough to seal. Cut roll-up in half to create two small pieces. Place rolls on ungreased cookie sheet. Bake at 375° for 11–13 minutes, until golden brown. Using a hot pad, remove pan from oven. Serve at once.

Yield: 8 pieces

Frozen Yogurt Apple Cups

Skill Level
beginner

Prep Time
8 minutes

Cook Time
none
(1 hour in freezer)

Equipment
spoon
paper cups
plastic spoons

Layered applesauce and yogurt makes a frozen treat that is rich and creamy but not too sweet.

1 8-ounce container fruit-flavored yogurt
1/2 cup applesauce

Stir yogurt until it is smooth and the fruit is completely mixed into the yogurt. In four small paper cups, spoon a layer of yogurt. Top with a layer of applesauce. Repeat layers until cups are filled to the top. Freeze until just firm, about 1 hour. Eat with a spoon.

Yield: 4 servings

Cheese Quesadillas

Skill Level
intermediate

Prep Time
10 minutes

Cook Time
8–10 minutes

Equipment
cheese grater
skillet
paring knife
cutting board
spatula
hot mitt

Quesadillas are a delicious Mexican snack food made with flour tortillas and melted cheese. To jazz them up, add extra toppings.

2 6-inch flour tortillas
1/2 cup shredded cheddar cheese
baking spray

Garnishes:
chopped onion   *chopped tomato*
diced green pepper   *crumbled bacon*
jalapeño peppers   *sour cream*
salsa

Lay flour tortillas flat. Top one tortilla with the shredded cheddar cheese. Add any of the optional toppings listed above. Top with the second tortilla.

Spray a large skillet with baking spray. Place the filled quesadilla in the skillet. Cook over medium high heat for about 4–6 minutes per side, or until lightly browned.

Using a spatula, carefully transfer the quesadilla to a serving plate. Cut into wedges as you would a pizza. Good plain or garnish each wedge with sour cream and salsa.

Yield: 1–2 servings

COOK'S CORNER
Cooked onion tastes milder than raw onion. To cook, place the chopped onion and 1 teaspoon butter in a microwave-safe dish. Microwave on high for about 2 minutes or until soft. Sprinkle the cooked onion over the cheese before cooking the quesadilla.

Flying Pizza Saucers

Skill Level
intermediate

Prep Time
10 minutes

Cook Time
10 minutes

Equipment
cutting board
paring knife
cheese grater
spatula

The name doesn't mean you'll be tossing your pizza around in a food fight. It means this pizza tastes so good it will fly off the dish and into your mouth. Happy eating!

1 English muffin
4 Tablespoons bottled spaghetti or pizza sauce
1/4 cup shredded mozzarella cheese
2 Tablespoons Parmesan cheese
dash oregano or basil, to taste

Optional toppings:
chopped tomato   *chopped zucchini*
sliced pepperoni   *chopped onion*
sliced mushrooms   *diced green pepper*
cooked sausage

Preheat oven to 350°.

Slice English muffin in half. Place the two halves on a baking sheet. Top each muffin half with 2 Tablespoons tomato sauce. Sprinkle each with mozzarella cheese and Parmesan cheese. Add optional toppings to taste. Sprinkle with oregano or basil.

Bake at 350° for 8–10 minutes, until cheese bubbles and muffins looks crusty around the edges. Using a hot pad, remove the baking sheet from oven. Use a spatula to transfer pizzas to serving plates. Serve warm.

Variation: Toast the English muffin halves, assemble pizzas as directed and microwave for 1–2 minutes

Yield: 2 servings

Waffle Club Sandwich

Skill Level
beginner

Prep Time
10 minutes

Cook Time
3 minutes

Equipment
toaster
knife
toothpicks

Frozen breakfast waffles are the "bread" in this unusual club sandwich. Served with a glass of milk, it is hearty enough to be a meal instead of a snack.

3 frozen waffles
3 Tablespoons peanut butter
1 small banana, sliced
2 Tablespoons marshmallow creme
3 Tablespoons jelly or jam, any flavor
2 Tablespoons raisins
2 Tablespoons chocolate chips
2 Tablespoons shredded coconut, optional

Toast frozen waffles as directed on box.

Spread one toasted waffle with peanut butter. Top with sliced banana. Sprinkle with raisins. Spread second waffle with marshmallow creme. Top with jelly or jam. Sprinkle with chocolate chips and coconut.

To assemble, top the peanut butter waffle with the marshmallow-jelly waffle. Top with the third waffle. Put a toothpick in each of the four corners of the waffle sandwich so it won't fall apart. Carefully cut into fourths. To serve, place the sandwich wedges on a plate with the fillings facing up.

Yield: 1 serving

Sleepovers, Club Meetings and Parties

There are lots of chances to get together with friends—projects, scouts, clubs or sports. Or you may enjoy having a few friends over to play games, watch a movie or spend the night. Whenever people get together, it is nice to have something special to eat or drink. While the food is never as important as the people, it's still fun to plan and serve snacks you think your guests will enjoy. Pick out and master a dish or two with your own special touches. Share them with pride the next time you host a sleepover, club meeting or party. When you plan for a gathering, remember to assemble all the serving dishes, glasses and silverware and set them out ahead of time. That way, you can serve with the cool, calm style of a practiced host or hostess.

Saucy Dogs

Skill Level
beginner

Prep Time
5 minutes

Cook Time
3 minutes

Equipment
*paring knife
cutting board
measuring cups
microwave dish
large spoon
hot pad*

Here's a hot snack for cold winter days. Serve in a bowl with lots of napkins—they are deliciously messy!

*4 hot dogs
1/4 cup grape jelly
1/4 cup chili sauce*

Cut each hot dog into 5 or 6 chunks.

In a microwave-safe casserole dish, combine grape jelly and chili sauce. Using a large spoon, stir the sauce until smooth. Microwave on high for 1 minute. Stir the sauce, then add the hot dog chunks and stir to coat each piece.

Microwave on high for 3 minutes, or until hot. Using a hot pad, remove dish from microwave. To serve, use toothpicks to spear hot dog chunks. Keep a napkin handy!

Party Dogs: For a party, substitute a package of fancy cocktail size all-beef franks for the hot dogs. Cook as directed above and serve in a shallow bowl with a toothpick inserted into each mini-frank.

Yield: 2 servings

Yummy Yogurt Dip

Skill Level
beginner

Prep Time
15 minutes

Cook Time
none

Equipment
mixing bowl
spoon
paring knife
cutting board
toothpicks

This delicious dip can be served with any type of fruit. A variety of fruits makes a colorful party platter that is sure to be a hit.

Yogurt Dip
1 8-ounce carton fruit flavored yogurt
1/2 cup frozen dessert topping, thawed
2 Tablespoons sugar
1 teaspoon vanilla, optional

Fruit for Dipping
Use any or all of the following:
2 apples
2 bananas
2 oranges
1 large bunch seedless grapes
1 8-ounce can pineapple chunks, drained
1 10.5-ounce can mandarin oranges, drained

In a small mixing bowl combine the yogurt, thawed dessert topping, sugar and vanilla. Stir with a spoon until combined and creamy. Refrigerate until serving time.

Use any combination of fruits for dipping. Wash apples and cut into wedges, being sure to remove the seeds. Cut bananas into 1-inch chunks. Peel oranges, removing as much white pith as possible. Separate into wedges. Wash grapes and separate into small bunches. For pineapple and mandarin oranges, open the cans and drain off liquid.

To serve, put the yogurt dip into a small dish in the center of a large plate. Surround with the various types of fruit. Provide decorative spears or toothpicks for dipping.

Yield: 8–10 servings

Cheesy Pepper Popcorn

Skill Level
intermediate

Prep Time
15 minutes

Cook Time
10 minutes to bake

Equipment
*microwave dish
measuring spoons
large bowl
wooden spoon
hot pads*

If you like popcorn and spicy food, this is the perfect combination for you. Use more or less chili powder to suit your taste.

*2 bags butter flavor microwave popcorn
  (8 cups popped)
4 Tablespoons butter
1 Tablespoon grated Romano cheese
1 teaspoon Italian herb seasoning
1/2 teaspoon paprika
1/4 teaspoon chili powder
1/8 teaspoon ground red pepper*

Preheat oven to 200°.

Pop each bag of microwave popcorn according to the directions on the package. Set aside to cool.

Place butter in a large microwave-safe dish. Microwave on high for 1 minute, or until melted. Remove from microwave and add the Romano cheese, Italian seasoning, paprika, chili powder and red pepper. Stir to mix.

Place the popped corn in a large mixing bowl and pour the butter mixture on top. Stir and toss the popcorn with a wooden spoon or clean hands until well coated.

Spread the popcorn mixture in a large shallow pan. Bake at 200° for 10 minutes. Store any leftovers in an air-tight container.

Yield: 8 cups

Chili Con Queso

Skill Level
intermediate

Prep Time
10 minutes

Cook Time
2–3 minutes

Equipment
measuring cups
wooden spoon
microwave dish
serving plate

This is an easy version of a classic Mexican hot cheese dip. If you like your dip extra spicy, add a few drops of hot sauce or substitute hot salsa for the mild.

1/2 cup chopped onions
1/2 cup chopped green peppers
1/2 cup mild salsa
8 ounces mild Mexican flavor processed cheese
tortilla chips

In a medium size microwave-safe dish, place onions, peppers, and salsa. Microwave for 1 minute, or until vegetables are soft.

Place the block of cheese on a cutting board and slice into small chunks. Add to the vegetable mixture. Microwave on high for one minute. Stir. If cheese is not melted, continue to cook in 30 second intervals until hot and melted through. Using hot pads, carefully remove from the oven.

To serve, place the bowl of dip on a large serving platter and surround with tortilla chips.

Yield: 2-1/2 cups

Spike's Spicy Snack Mix

Skill Level
intermediate

Prep Time
15 minutes

Cook Time
oven, 20–30 minutes;
microwave, 6 minutes

Equipment
measuring cup
measuring spoon
wooden spoon
hot pads
cookie sheets

The next time you invite friends over to watch a movie or play a board game, surprise them with this special snack mix.

baking spray
1 Tablespoon worcestershire sauce
6 Tablespoons butter
1/2 teaspoon curry powder
1/2 teaspoon instant onion flakes
1/8 teaspoon garlic powder
1 cup wheat squares cereal
1 cup rice squares cereal
1 cup oat circles cereal
1 cup goldfish or small cheese crackers
1 cup thin pretzel sticks
1/2 cup sunflower seeds or pine nuts, toasted
1/2 cup roasted peanuts

Preheat oven to 300°. Spray two cookie sheets with baking spray and set aside.

In a small saucepan over medium heat, place the worcestershire sauce, butter, curry powder, onion flakes and garlic powder. Cook for 2–3 minutes, or until butter melts and you can smell the spices.

Place cereal, crackers, pretzels and nuts in a large mixing bowl, stirring to combine. Gently pour the butter mixture over cereal mixture. Using a large wooden spoon, stir until the snack mix is well combined and evenly coated.

Spread half the cereal mixture on each cookie sheet. Bake at 300° for 20 to 30 minutes. Using hot pads, carefully remove the cookie sheets from the oven. Allow mixture to cool before serving. Store leftovers in an air-tight container.

Yield: 6 cups

Stuffed Celery Circles

Skill Level
beginner

Prep Time
15 minutes

Cook Time
none

Equipment
cutting board
knife
plastic wrap

It doesn't take much longer to make celery circles than the usual stuffed celery sticks, but they have two advantages. They're more interesting looking and are a convenient bite-sized nibble.

6 stalks celery
1 3-ounce package of cream cheese with chives, at room temperature
sliced olives or parsley, for garnish

Wash the celery stalks, and trim off the top and bottom ends.

Fill each stalk with cream cheese. Place one stalk of celery on top of another, filled sides facing (try to match up celery stalks of similar size and diameter). Wrap the three stuffed logs in clear plastic wrap and refrigerate for an hour. To serve, cut into bite-sized slices. Garnish each piece with a slice of olive or a piece of parsley, if desired.

To vary this snack, use any filling you like such as cream cheese and pineapple, ham spread, or peanut butter. Or, stuff and slice other vegetables such as hollowed out cucumber or zucchini.

Yield: about 24 slices

Golden Globe Cheese Ball

Skill Level
intermediate

Prep Time
20 minutes

Cook Time
none

Equipment
cutting board
knife
mixing bowl
electric mixer

Serve this cheese ball on a pretty plate, surrounded by various types of plain or fancy crackers. It is sure to become a favorite.

1 lb. cheddar cheese, grated
1 lb. block pasteurized processed cheese spread, cut into chunks
1 8-ounce package cream cheese, at room temperature
2 teaspoons worcestershire sauce
2 teaspoons chopped onion
6 Tablespoons milk
chopped parsley or chopped nuts, for garnish
assorted crackers

Set out all the ingredients for 15 minutes at room temperature to allow cheeses to soften and milk to warm up a bit for easier mixing.

In a large bowl, combine all ingredients. Using an electric mixer, beat until smooth and well combined. Using damp hands, shape mixture into three balls or three small logs. Chill 2–3 hours or until firm.

To garnish, place chopped parsley or chopped nuts on a sheet of waxed paper. Roll the cheese balls or logs in the garnish. Place on a platter. Serve with crackers.

Yield: 3 cheese balls or logs

Cranberry Orange Zinger

Skill Level
beginner

Prep Time
20 minutes

Cook Time
none

Equipment
measuring cups
large pitcher
spoon

Serve this festive drink for a change from soda.

2 cups of orange juice
2 cups cranberry juice
1 liter of ginger ale

Mix all ingredients in a large pitcher. Stir well and chill until serving time. To serve, pour the punch over ice in a punch bowl. Or, pour from a pitcher into glasses filled with ice.

Yield: 20 one half cup servings

Tropical Punch

Skill Level
beginner

Prep Time
20 minutes

Cook Time
none

Equipment
measuring cups
large pitcher
spoon
can opener

Serve this punch at your next party.

1 package of lime flavored powdered drink mix
4 cups water
1 cup sugar, or to taste
1 46-ounce can of pineapple juice
1 liter carbonated lemon-lime drink

Mix all ingredients in a large container. Stir well and chill until serving time. To serve, place ice cubes or an ice ring in a punch bowl and pour in the punch. Or, pour from a pitcher into glasses filled with ice.

Yield: 30 one half cup servings

Family Favorites

Cooking for the family is the backbone of all cooking—after all, we have to eat every day. Whether you are preparing an entire meal, or helping out by making muffins, salad or dessert you'll be doing it for your most deserving and appreciative audience—your family.

Cooking with the family is a way to practice your skills and learn new ones. It is also fun to spend time with other family members in the kitchen. This chapter includes recipes that may soon become your family's favorites.

French Toast Surprise

Skill Level
intermediate

Prep Time
10 minutes

Cook Time
12–15 minutes

Equipment
mixing bowl
measuring cups
measuring
*   spoons*
spreader
shallow dish
skillet
hot pad
whisk or fork

What a pleasant surprise to find a creamy, sweet layer of strawberries and cream cheese in the middle of your French toast!

4 Tablespoons strawberry preserves
1 3-ounce package cream cheese, at room
*   temperature*
8 slices white bread
4 eggs beaten
1/4 cup milk
2 teaspoons sugar
1/2 teaspoon vanilla extract
4 Tablespoons butter, divided
2 teaspoons confectioner's sugar

Place the strawberry preserves and cream cheese in a small mixing bowl. Stir well to combine. Spread the mixture over four of the slices of bread. Top each with a second slice of bread to make a sandwich.

In a shallow dish, combine the eggs, milk, sugar and vanilla extract. Beat well with a fork or whisk. Dip each sandwich into the egg, coating both sides.

In a large non-stick skillet, melt 2 tablespoons butter. Cook the first two sandwiches for about three minutes or until lightly browned on the bottom. Flip sandwiches over and continue cooking until other sides are lightly browned. Using a spatula, remove the sandwiches from the skillet and cover with aluminum foil to keep warm. Melt another 2 tablespoons butter in the skillet and cook the next two sandwiches the same way.

To serve, sprinkle French toast with powdered sugar and top with maple syrup if desired.

Yield: 4 servings

Peanut Butter and Jelly Buns

Skill Level
intermediate

Prep Time
5 minutes

Cook Time
8–10 minutes

Equipment
spoon
fork
baking sheet

These rolls feature the favorite taste combination of peanut butter and jelly in a roll. They are delicious for breakfast, or for a family dessert.

1 10-ounce package flaky refrigerated biscuits
5 Tablespoons smooth peanut butter
5 Tablespoons jam or jelly, any flavor

Preheat oven to 400°.

Open can and separate the 10 biscuits. Divide each biscuit in half to make a total of 20 pieces of dough. Place a half teaspoon of peanut butter in the center of 10 biscuits. Top each with a second biscuit. Using a fork, press down on the edges of each biscuit, to seal the peanut butter inside.

Place biscuits 2 inches apart on an ungreased baking sheet. Using your thumb, make a deep imprint in the center of each biscuit. Fill the imprint with a half teaspoon of jelly or jam (be careful not to use too much or it will overflow during baking).

Bake at 400° for 8-10 minutes, or as directed on package, until golden brown. Using a hot pad, carefully remove from oven. Let biscuits cool for several minutes before serving—the jelly will be very hot so don't burn your mouth!

Yield: 10 buns

Toasty Cheese Sandwich

Skill Level
intermediate

Prep Time
4 minutes

Cook Time
6 to 8 minutes

Equipment
skillet
butter spreader
spatula
hot pads

A simple combination of bread and cheese grilled in a skillet is a satisfying sandwich. Some people like to "gild the lily" by adding meat and pickles.

1 Tablespoon butter, softened
2 slices of bread (your choice)
1 slice American cheese

Butter two pieces of bread. Place the cheese between the two slices of bread, butter sides facing out.

Heat a skillet for one minute over medium heat. Place sandwich in skillet and let it cook for about 2–3 minutes, or until brown on the bottom. Using a spatula, flip the sandwich over and cook the second side. This side will cook faster. Transfer the sandwich to a serving plate. Cut in half and serve at once.

Gilded Lily Toasted Cheese Sandwich:
Assemble the sandwich as directed above, adding a slice of ham or bologna, pickle chips and mayonnaise or mustard. Cook as directed.

Yield: 1 sandwich

COOK'S CORNER
If you are not allowed to use a skillet, try this microwave version. Toast two pieces of bread in a toaster. Place 1 slice of cheese between the two pieces of toast. Put on a microwave-safe dish. Microwave for 30 seconds, or until cheese melts.

Croque Monsieur

Skill Level
intermediate

Prep Time
8 minutes

Cook Time
6–8 minutes

Equipment
*sandwich
  spreader
shallow dish
fork or whisk
skillet
spatula
hot pads*

This French sandwich is frequently ordered by tourists at sidewalk cafes in Paris. Enjoy a similar treat without ever leaving home.

*2 slices of French or Italian bread
1 teaspoon Dijon style mustard
1 slice cooked ham
1 slice Swiss or Gruyere cheese
2 slices dill pickle, optional
1 egg
2 Tablespoons butter*

Assemble the sandwich by spreading one slice of bread with mustard. Top with ham and then cheese. Add pickle slices and top with the other slice of bread.

In a shallow dish large enough to hold the sandwich (a pie plate is perfect), beat an egg with a fork or whisk. Carefully dip sandwich into beaten egg, turning to coat both sides.

Melt 2 tablespoons butter in a large skillet over medium heat. Place sandwich in skillet and cook 3 to 4 minutes, or until lightly browned on the bottom. Using a spatula, flip the sandwich over to cook the second side— it will cook faster. When toasted on both sides, transfer the sandwich to a serving plate. To serve, cut in half.

Junior Croque Monsieur: Toast two slices of frozen french toast in a toaster. Spread one slice with mustard. Top with ham, cheese and pickle. Top with second slice of french toast. Place on a microwave-safe dish and microwave on high for 1 minute, or until cheese melts.

Yield: 1 sandwich

Roast Chicken Fajitas

Skill Level
intermediate

Prep Time
*10 minutes for
    meat plus
    marinating
    time
15 minutes for
    garnishes*

Cook Time
*15–30 seconds
    for tortilla
3 minutes for
    chicken*

Equipment
*plastic bag
measuring cups
measuring
    spoons
microwave dish*

Everyone enjoys fajitas. This version features pre-roasted chicken for an authentic taste without having to fire up a grill.

*1/4 cup chicken broth
1 Tablespoon olive oil
1/2 teaspoon cumin
2 Tablespoons lime juice
1/4 teaspoon oregano
1/4 teaspoon minced garlic
1 teaspoon soy sauce
3 green onions, finely sliced
2 roasted chicken breasts
1 small onion, coarsely chopped
1 small green pepper, coarsely chopped
8 6-inch flour tortillas*

Optional Garnishes:
*shredded lettuce   shredded cheese
mild or hot salsa   sour cream*

Place chicken broth, olive oil, cumin, lime juice, oregano, garlic, soy sauce, green onions and chicken breasts in a one-gallon size reclosable plastic bag. Shake it to mix up the ingredients. Place bag in refrigerator for at least one hour. Remove chicken from bag and discard marinade. With clean hands or a paring knife, shred the meat. Place chicken in a microwave-safe dish. Add green pepper and onion. Cook on high 3-4 minutes until chicken is warm and vegetables are soft.

Microwave tortillas for 15 to 30 seconds. Wrap in paper towels, then in aluminum foil to keep them warm. To serve, place chicken mixture and selected garnishes in the tortilla. Fold in half or roll it up.

Yield: 8 servings

Oriental Chicken Salad

Skill Level
intermediate

Prep Time
20 minutes

Cook Time
3 minutes

Equipment
microwave-safe
*   bowl*
hot pads
measuring cup
measuring
*   spoons*
mixing bowls
whisk or fork

The combination of crisp and creamy plus nutty and crunchy has everything a good salad should have. Your parents will think you are a gourmet cook.

1 chicken breast
1 teaspoon lemon juice
1/8 teaspoon minced garlic
1/2 cup Italian salad dressing
1 1/2 Tablespoons sugar
3 Tablespoons peanut butter
1 Tablespoon soy sauce
1/4 teaspoon dried red pepper
2 cups thinly sliced cabbage
1 carrot, grated
1/2 cup frozen peas, defrosted
1/2 cup thinly sliced sweet green pepper
4 green onions, including tops, thinly sliced
1/2 cup diced celery
1 8-ounce can sliced water chestnuts, drained

Place chicken in a microwave safe bowl. Sprinkle with lemon juice and minced garlic. Cover and microwave 1 to 2 minutes, until chicken is cooked through. Using kitchen scissors or a knife, slice the meat into shreds. Drain off juices, and place in refrigerator to chill.

To make the dressing, in a small bowl combine the Italian dressing, sugar, peanut butter, soy sauce and pepper. Beat with a whisk or fork until smooth.

In a large mixing bowl, combine sliced cabbage, grated carrot, frozen peas, green pepper, green onions, celery and water chestnuts. Stir gently to mix all ingredients.

To serve, divide the salad mixture between two plates. Top each salad with half the chicken strips. Drizzle peanut dressing over each salad.

Yield: 2 main dish or 4 side dish servings

Easy Italian Lasagna

Skill Level
intermediate

Prep Time
30 minutes

Cook Time
*15–45 minutes,
depending
upon cooking
method*

Equipment
*8×8×2 inch
baking dish
hot pads
mixing bowls
measuring cup
measuring
spoons
fork or whisk*

No-boil lasagna is a special type of noodle that doesn't have to be pre-cooked before the casserole is assembled.

*1 egg
1 cup ricotta cheese
1 lb. ground hamburger meat
1/2 teaspoon basil
1 teaspoon oregano
1/2 teaspoon garlic, or more to taste
baking spray
1 30-ounce jar spaghetti sauce
6 no-boil lasagna noodles
2 cups shredded mozzarella
1/2 cup grated Parmesan cheese*

In a small mixing bowl, beat the egg with a fork. Stir in the ricotta cheese and set aside.

In a large mixing bowl, mix hamburger meat with basil, oregano and garlic. Using clean, wet hands, make tiny meatballs about the size of large marbles, using all the meat mixture. Place meatballs on waxed paper and set aside.

Spray an 8×8×2 inch microwave-safe baking pan with baking spray. Cover bottom of pan with 1/2 cup of spaghetti sauce. Top sauce with no-boil lasagna noodles, being careful it doesn't touch sides of pan. Cover the noodles with one third of the ricotta cheese mixture. Top with one third of the tiny meat balls. Cover meatballs with one third of the mozzarella cheese. Top with 1/2 cup spaghetti sauce. Sprinkle generously with Parmesan cheese. Make two more layers.

Cover with plastic wrap, leaving one edge open for a vent. Microwave on high for 15–20 minutes, rotating dish after every 5 minutes. Or, bake at 350° in a conventional oven for 30–40 minutes. Let stand 5 minutes before cutting.

Yield: 4 servings

Creamed Chipped Beef

Skill Level
beginner

Prep Time
10 minutes

Equipment
*microwave-safe
  bowl*
hot pads
measuring cup
*measuring
  spoons*
can opener
knife
cutting board

This dish can be served any time of the day. Without the vegetables, it makes a nourishing breakfast served over toast or waffles. Do not add salt to this dish since dried beef is very salty.

baking spray
1 Tablespoon butter
3 Tablespoons diced onion
3 Tablespoons diced green pepper
1/2 cup frozen green peas
1 10 3/4 ounce can cream of mushroom soup
1/4 cup milk
8 ounces dried chipped beef
toast, waffles, biscuits or rice

Spray a large microwave-safe bowl or casserole dish with baking spray. Add 1 tablespoon butter, diced onion, green pepper and the peas. Microwave on high for 1 to 2 minutes, or until vegetables are softened and cooked.

Using hot pads, remove bowl from microwave oven. Add soup and milk. Stir until well mixed. Using clean hands or kitchen scissors, shred the beef into the soup mixture. Stir well.

Return bowl to microwave and cook for 2–3 minutes. Rotate the bowl and stir after each minute. To serve, spoon the creamed chipped beef over toast, waffles, biscuits or rice.

Variation: If you prefer, substitute cream of celery soup for the cream of mushroom soup.

Yield: 4 servings

Fish Fillets Italian Style

Skill Level
intermediate

Prep Time
15 minutes

Cook Time
5–6 minutes

Equipment
*microwave dish
hot pads
mixing bowl
table knife
fork*

This Italian-style fish dish is made in record time in the microwave oven. Add cole slaw from the delicatessen and bread for a quick and nutritious meal.

*baking spray
1 pound flounder or sole fish fillets
3 Tablespoons butter
1 Tablespoon lemon juice
lemon pepper or fresh ground pepper, to taste
1/2 cup mayonnaise
1/4 teaspoon oregano
2 Tablespoons dried onion flakes
3 Tablespoons grated Parmesan cheese
paprika*

Spray a microwave safe dish with baking spray. Place fish in the prepared baking dish. Dot the fish with butter, drizzle on lemon juice, and sprinkle with pepper.

Cover fish with waxed paper and microwave for 2 minutes. Using hot pads, carefully remove from the microwave. Set aside.

In a small mixing bowl, combine mayonnaise, oregano, onion and Parmesan cheese. Using a table knife, spread the mayonnaise mixture evenly over the fish filets. Sprinkle with paprika. Return to microwave for 2 to 3 minutes, checking after each minute. The fish will flake with a fork when it is done.

Chicken Breasts Italian Style: Substitute 1 pound boneless chicken breasts for the fish.

Yield: 4 servings

Super Supper Stroganoff

Skill Level
intermediate

Prep Time
10 minutes

Cook Time
8–10 minutes

Equipment
microwave dish
knife
cutting board
spoon
hot pads
measuring cup
measuring
  spoons

This is a homey version of an old favorite.

baking spray
4 green onions, sliced
1/4 cup diced celery, optional
1/4 teaspoon minced garlic
1/4 cup green pepper, optional
1 3-ounce can sliced mushrooms, drained
1 Tablespoon butter
1 teaspoon soy sauce
1 teaspoon mustard
2 Tablespoons ketchup
1/2 pound ground beef
1 6-ounce package egg noodles
1 10 3/4 ounce can cream of mushroom soup
1/2 cup beef broth

Spray a large microwave safe baking dish with baking spray. Add green onions, celery, garlic, green pepper, mushrooms and 1 tablespoon butter. Microwave on high for 1 minute. Add soy sauce, mustard, ketchup, and ground beef. Stir to mix. Microwave 3 minutes. Stir.

Boil noodles according to package directions. Using a strainer, carefully drain water off the cooked noodles. Combine noodles, mushroom soup, and beef broth with beef mixture. Microwave for 3–6 minutes, until casserole is hot and beef is no longer pink. Stir casserole after each minute.

Special touches. For an extra-rich dish, stir in 2 tablespoons of sour cream. If you like, top the casserole with canned French fried onion rings, or shredded cheddar cheese.

Yield: 4–6 servings

Pepperoni and Cheese Stromboli

Skill Level
advanced

Prep Time
20 minutes

Cook Time
18 minutes

Equipment
baking sheet
microwave dish
mixing bowl
cutting board
knife
measuring cups
measuring
  spoons
fork or whisk
spoon

Stromboli is like rolled pizza, with the cheese and pepperoni inside the dough instead of on top.

baking spray
1 small onion, chopped
1 Tablespoon butter
1 egg
1/2 cup ricotta cheese
1 1/2 cups shredded mozzarella cheese
1/2 teaspoon dried oregano
1/2 teaspoon pepper
1 10-ounce package refrigerated pizza crust
1/2 pound sliced pepperoni
vegetable cooking spray or vegetable oil
1 Tablespoon water

Preheat oven to 400°. Coat a baking sheet with baking spray. Set aside.

Place chopped onion and 1 tablespoon butter in a microwave-safe dish. Microwave on high for 1–2 minutes

Break egg into a small mixing bowl. Beat with a fork or whisk. Add onion, ricotta cheese, mozzarella cheese, oregano and pepper. Stir well. Set aside.

Unroll pizza dough on a lightly floured surface. Handle carefully as the dough will stretch. Spoon cheese mixture over the dough in an even layer. Top with pepperoni slices. Using clean, damp hands, roll up the dough lengthwise to create a long roll. Place the stromboli on a baking sheet. Brush the top with water. Bake at 400° for 18 minutes or until golden brown. Using a hot pad, remove pan from oven. Cut into slices and top with tomato sauce, if desired.

Yield: 4–6 servings

One-Dish Chicken Supper

Skill Level
advanced

Prep Time
15 minutes

Cook Time
30 minutes

Equipment
3 quart shallow baking pan
mixing bowl
cutting board
knife
spoon
aluminum foil
hot pad

Rich gravy surrounds the chicken and stuffing in this one-dish meal. It's a perfect dish to serve guests because it can be made ahead.

1 10 3/4-ounce can cream of mushroom soup
1 14 1/2-ounce can chicken broth
1 12-ounce jar chicken gravy
1 6-ounce package chicken flavor stuffing mix
1/2 cup chopped carrots
1/2 cup chopped onion
1/2 cup chopped celery
3 skinless, boneless chicken breasts, cut in half

Preheat oven to 400°.

In a large bowl, combine mushroom soup, chicken broth and gravy. Stir until well combined. Set aside.

Prepare the stuffing mix according to package directions, adding the chopped carrots, onion and celery with the seasoning packet.

Spoon a thin layer of gravy mixture across the bottom of a large shallow baking dish. Pile the stuffing mixture across the center of dish. Place the chicken pieces on each side of stuffing, overlapping if necessary. Pour remaining gravy over the top of the chicken and stuffing. Cover dish with aluminum foil.

Place in preheated 400° oven. Bake 15 minutes. Using hot pads, carefully remove foil. Bake 15 minutes longer, or until dish looks hot and bubbly and chicken can be pierced easily with a fork. Using hot pads, carefully remove dish from oven.

Yield: 4 to 6 servings

Chili Corn Taters

Skill Level
beginner

Prep Time
10 minutes

Cook Time
*8 minutes
(potatoes)
3 minutes (chili
mixture)*

Equipment
*can opener
microwave dish
fork
spoon
hot pads*

Try this recipe for a fast and filling meal. When you have more time, make it with your own version of homemade chili.

*2 baking potatoes, well-scrubbed
1 15-ounce can chili with beans
1 cup of frozen corn or drained canned corn
2 teaspoons chopped mild green chili peppers
1/2 cup mild salsa
1/4 cup shredded Cheddar cheese*

Pierce each potato two or three times with a fork, to create steam vents. Place potatoes in microwave and cook on high for 4 minutes. Let stand for 2 minutes. Rotate the potatoes. Microwave for 4 more minutes. Pierce each potato with a fork to see if it is done (potato should pierce easily). If not, cook for 1–2 minutes longer. Set aside.

In a large microwave-safe dish, combine the chili, corn, chopped green chilies and salsa. Microwave on high for 3 minutes, stirring after 2 minutes.

To serve, cut each potato in half and place on a serving plate. Top each potato with half the chili mixture. Sprinkle half the Cheddar cheese on top of each potato.

Yield: 2 servings

Kicky Cole Slaw

Skill Level
intermediate

Prep Time
10 minutes

Cook Time
none

Equipment
can opener
mixing bowls
whisk
wooden spoon
measuring cup

This is cole slaw with a twist—the fruit cocktail makes it slightly sweet so it is a hit with kids of all ages.

2 cups sliced green cabbage
1 carrot, grated
1 16-ounce can fruit cocktail, save juice
1/4 cup shredded Cheddar cheese, optional

Dressing
1/4 cup mayonnaise
juice from 16-ounce can fruit cocktail

In a large mixing bowl, combine the sliced cabbage, grated carrot, drained fruit cocktail, and Cheddar cheese. Stir well with a wooden spoon. Set aside.

In a small mixing bowl, make the salad dressing by whisking together 1/4 cup mayonnaise and 2 tablespoons juice reserved from the fruit cocktail. If desired, add additional fruit juice to taste.

Pour the dressing over the salad a little at a time, stirring after each addition. Hint: too much dressing makes a soggy salad. Chill 30 minutes before serving.

Yield: 4 servings.

Light-As-A-Feather Biscuits

Skill Level
intermediate

Prep Time
10 minutes

Cook Time
6–8 minutes

Equipment
*measuring cups
measuring
    spoons
wooden spoon
rolling pin
hot pads
cookie sheet*

The best biscuits are the ones you make at home. Using a biscuit mix, you can bake a batch in no time at all.

*1 pkg rapid quick yeast
1 Tablespoon sugar
1/4 cup warm water
2 cups baking mix
1/4 cup milk*

In a medium bowl, dissolve the yeast and sugar in warm water (105° to 115° degrees), stirring to mix. Add baking mix and milk and stir to form a dough. Smooth into a ball.

On a counter top dusted with baking mix, knead the dough ten times. Using a rolling pin, roll the dough out 1/2 inch thick. Cut out biscuits with a 2″ biscuit cutter or small drinking glass.

Place the biscuits on an ungreased cookie sheet. Let rise in a warm place for 30 minutes. Preheat oven to 425°. Bake 6–8 minutes, or until golden brown.

Cinnamon Sugar Bits: Cut leftover biscuit scraps into small pieces. Roll in melted butter, then in a mixture of cinnamon and sugar. Let rise and bake as directed. Makes a nice light dessert or television snack!

Yield: 8–10 biscuits

Delicious Desserts

In England, students often ask "What's for afters?" They refer to desserts as "afters" because they come after the main course. Desserts are often an introduction to cooking as many people begin by making candy, cookies and cakes and then go on to other types of cooking. Learn to make a delicious dessert, then sit back to wait for the compliments!

Fruit Pizza

Skill Level
intermediate

Prep Time
15 minutes

Cook Time
15 minutes

Equipment
*pizza pan
cooking spray
large bowl
wooden spoon
pastry brush*

Fruit pizza is a sweet shortbread crust topped with a layer of cream and a bountiful assortment of fruit.

Crust
*baking spray
1 8-ounce box yellow cake mix
2 Tablespoons butter
2 Tablespoons water
1 egg*

Topping
*1 8-ounce container frozen whipped topping, thawed
1 pint whole strawberries, washed and sliced
1 bunch seedless white grapes
1 10-1/2-ounce can Mandarin oranges, drained
1 20-ounce can sliced pineapple
1 banana, sliced*

Glaze
*1/2 cup apricot preserves
2 Tablespoons water*

Preheat oven to 350°. Spray pizza pan with baking spray. Set aside. Combine cake mix, butter and water in a large bowl. Using an electric mixer, beat for two minutes. Batter will be stiff. Spread batter over the prepared pizza pan. Bake at 350° for 15 minutes. Let cool. Spread thawed whipped topping over the cake. Arrange fruit in a pretty design over the topping.

Heat apricot preserves and water in a small saucepan. Stir until smooth. Brush the glaze evenly over the top of the pizza. To serve, cut into wedges. Store in refrigerator.

Yield: 8–12 servings

Easy Microwave Fudge

Skill Level
advanced

Prep Time
10 minutes

Cook Time
1–3 minutes

Equipment
*8 × 8 baking
    pan
measuring cups
measuring
    spoons
medium glass
    bowl
knife*

Do you like fudge? Who doesn't! This recipe takes only a few minutes to make. Cut into squares and packaged in a pretty container, it makes a nice gift for a teacher or friend.

1 Tablespoon butter
1 12-ounce package semi-sweet chocolate chips
1 cup sweetened condensed milk
1 teaspoon vanilla extract
dash of salt
3 Tablespoons powdered sugar
1/2 cup chopped pecans or walnuts, optional

Butter an 8-inch square pan and set aside.

Place the chocolate chips in a medium glass bowl. Microwave on medium power for 1 minute. Stir. If not completely melted, microwave for 30 seconds at a time until all the chocolate chips have melted.

Stir in the sweetened condensed milk, vanilla and salt. Add powdered sugar and nuts. Stir until well mixed—mixture will be very stiff.

Pour fudge into the buttered dish. Refrigerate until firm. To serve, cut into small pieces. Store in an air-tight container.

Yield: 1 pound fudge

COOK'S CORNER
Microwaved chocolate chips hold their shape even after they have melted. This is because chocolate chips contain a small amount of edible wax. Cook just until they look shiny. They will dissolve when stirred with a spoon.

Crazy Cobbler

Skill Level
intermediate

Prep Time
10 minutes

Cook Time
40–45 minutes

Equipment
*9 × 13 baking
  pan
can opener
wooden spoon
knife
hot pads
microwave-safe
  dish*

This cobbler combines dry cake mix with fruit and toppings for a perfect dessert to feed a crowd.

2 20-ounce cans cherry pie filling
1 15 1/4-ounce can crushed pineapple
1 18.25 ounce yellow cake mix, dry
1/2 cup coconut, optional
1 cup chopped nuts, optional
1/2 cup butter
ice cream or whipped cream, optional

Preheat oven to 350°.

Open two cans of cherry pie filling and pour both into a 9 × 13 baking pan. Open the can of crushed pineapple. Drain off any excess juice, then pour pineapple on top of cherries. Using a wooden spoon, swirl the cherries and pineapple together. Sprinkle fruit mixture with the box of dry yellow cake mix. Sprinkle with the coconut and/or chopped nuts.

Place butter in a microwave-safe dish. Microwave on high for 1 minute, or until melted. Drizzle the butter evenly over the top of the cobbler. Bake at 350° for 40 to 45 minutes, until lightly browned. Using a hot pad, remove pan from oven. Let cool for 15 minutes.

To serve, cut into squares and serve in shallow bowls—it will be juicy. Top each serving with a scoop of vanilla ice cream

Yield: 8–12 servings

Peanut Butter Cookies

Skill Level
intermediate

Prep Time
15 minutes

Cook Time
*10 minutes per
batch*

Equipment
*large mixing
bowl
measuring cups
wooden spoon
cookie sheets
hot pad
spatula*

Everyone loves peanut butter, especially in a cookie. These will disappear fast!

*1 cup butter, softened
1 cup brown sugar
1 cup white sugar
2 eggs
1 cup smooth peanut butter
3 cups flour
1 teaspoon baking soda*

Preheat oven to 350°.

In a large bowl, place the butter, brown sugar and white sugar. Using clean hands or a wooden spoon, cream together until mixture is smooth. Add eggs and peanut butter. Stir well. Add the flour and baking soda. Mix well.

Using clean hands, roll the cookie dough into 1-inch balls and place them two inches apart on an ungreased cookie sheet. Flatten each cookie by pressing down with the tines of a fork, first vertically and then horizontally, to make a criss-cross pattern.

Bake the cookies at 350° for 10 minutes. Using a hot pad, remove the cookie sheet from the oven. Use a spatula to remove the cookies from the cookie sheet onto a large plate. Continue baking batches of cookies until all the dough has been used.

Chocolate Kiss Cookies: Press an unwrapped chocolate kiss into the center of each cookie as soon as they are removed from oven. Allow cookies to cool completely before serving.

Yield: about 3 dozen cookies

Fantasy Brownie Bars

Skill Level
intermediate

Prep Time
15 minutes

Cook Time
25–30 minutes

Equipment
mixing bowl
wooden spoon
measuring cups
9 × 13 baking
  pan
hot pads

These are called fantasy bars because they combine lots of favorite ingredients into one incredibly delicious and sweet cookie bar.

1 21.5-ounce package brownie mix
1/2 cup chocolate chips
1/2 cup butterscotch chips
1 cup mini-marshmallows
1/2 cup flaked coconut, optional
1 cup chopped pecans, optional

Preheat oven to 350°.

Prepare brownie mix as directed on the box. Spread into a prepared pan. Bake at 350° for 20 minutes. Remove pan from oven. Sprinkle top of brownies with an even layer of chocolate chips, followed by butterscotch chips and mini-marshmallows. Sprinkle with coconut and/or chopped nuts. Pat the mixture down firmly into the brownies.

Bake at 350° for another 5 to 10 minutes, until marshmallows are lightly browned. Using a hot pad, remove pan from the oven. Cool one hour before cutting. Cut into 24 bars. Store the cookie bars loosely covered in the refrigerator or at room temperature.

Yield: 24 cookie bars

Holiday Sugar Cookies

Skill Level
advanced

Prep Time
*20 minutes
plus chilling
time*

Cook Time
*12 minutes per
batch*

Equipment
*electric mixer
mixing bowl
plastic wrap
rolling pin
cookie sheets
spatula*

Make a batch of these cookies for any holiday. Decorate the baked cookies with tubes of decorator icing, or with colored sugar.

*1 1/2 cups butter, at room temperature
1 cup granulated sugar
1 large egg
1 teaspoon vanilla extract
1/2 teaspoon salt
4 cups all-purpose flour
tubes of decorator icing, optional
colored sugar or sprinkles, optional*

Place the butter and sugar in a large bowl. Using an electric mixer, beat until creamy. Beat in the egg, vanilla and salt. At low speed, gradually add the flour until well blended. Divide the dough in half, wrap in plastic wrap and refrigerate for 1 hour or until firm.

Preheat oven to 375°. Have two or three ungreased cookie sheets ready.

On a clean, lightly floured counter top or large cutting board, roll out half of dough to a thickness of 1/4″. Cut out shapes with floured cookie cutters. Using a large spatula, carefully transfer the dough onto cookie sheets. Repeat with second batch of dough.

Bake cookies at 375° for 12 minutes or until edges start to brown. Using a hot pad, remove cookie sheets from oven. Use a spatula to transfer the cookies to wire racks to cool completely.

Yield: 4 dozen cookies

Mama Lee's Alabama Sundae Pie

Skill Level
beginner

Prep Time
25 minutes

Cook Time
none

Equipment
*large mixing
 bowl
measuring cups
spoon
spatula
cutting board
knife
plastic wrap*

This easy-as-pie recipe is always a hit with sundae lovers of all ages.

*1/4 cup sugar
4 ounces whipped cream cheese
1 9-inch prepared graham cracker pie crust
2 bananas
1 8-ounce can crushed pineapple, well drained
4 ounces frozen whipped topping, thawed*

Garnishes:
*chocolate syrup
chopped nuts
maraschino cherries*

In a small mixing bowl, combine sugar and cream cheese. Mix well. Spread over bottom of prepared pie crust.

Peel and slice the bananas. Layer banana slices over cream cheese, overlapping as needed. Top with crushed pineapple. Top with whipped topping. Cover with plastic wrap and freeze overnight, or until firm.

Remove from freezer 15 minutes before serving. Garnish whole pie or individual slices with chocolate syrup, chopped nuts and cherries.

Yield: 6–8 servings

 S0-CWV-477

Gleb...the Terrible!

Ten years have passed
since Jacky told his story. Cranky and
past his prime, he's ruled for seventeen years
– and now he's the only Blue left.
The coyotes got beautiful Rare, and Tom
and Kit have passed on from old age.
Girly Rune Tijous went the same way.
The household is full
of a different assortment of cats, and the
following account is from the perspective
of its latest addition...

Mrs. Anderzij was nice...
I was bewildered
by all the near-misses with cars and trains,

wandering through the underground metro
when she picked me up and took me home...
Her gentle hands and sweet voice
**told me that I was
safe at last...**

It was a relief
to meet someone kind for a change,
and I soon learned that she gave sanctuary
to seven more of us castoffs...

Yep – *she ran a real cat shelter –*
more like a zoo!

Her husband was from
the old country.
He read and chattered constantly in languages I didn't
understand, but he sure didn't know cat lingo
like Mrs. A. He used to tease me
about the little white patch on my tail –
he called it a "worry spot" – and he named me
after a Slavic saint.

It took a saint to put up with
all the ridicule I had to suffer
at his hands!

Their apartment in the city
was roomy enough for all of us, I guess.
But I'm a pretty husky fellow, with long, thick
legs and super-sized paws –
and oh, how I do
love to run and play!

I never meant to upset things or disturb their
tranquil ways, but I know I got on their nerves
with my energy explosions...

After a while, I began to hear
exasperated sighs,
then angry reproaches:

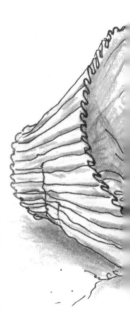

**"Gleb, don't do that!
Get out of there, Gleb!**

Gleb, did you break this?
Gleb, your big, clumsy feet
are s-o-o-o noisy!"

...and some very uncharitable comments...

"Ha! Ha! Yes, Gleb is our dumbest cat... he's so funny!
He does the strangest things... we suspect
he's got a disability...

Gleb? Oh, we think he might be
retarded...."

So... when Mr. and Mrs. Anderzij
moved to a new place
in an upscale neighborhood
that had a limit of five cats to a unit,
it came as no surprise to find out I wouldn't be going
with them...

But – sometimes
a disappointment is for the best.

Mrs. A took me
to her Mom's house –

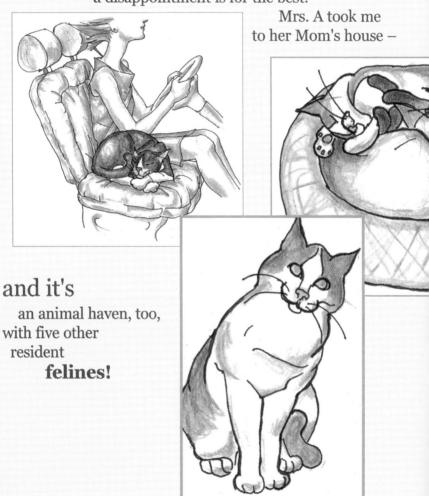

and it's
an animal haven, too,
with five other
resident
felines!

...There are the tabby twins:
Iris and **Olive**. Iris is very attractive,
a little on the plump side, so she makes a pretty good
cushion (or blanket) for His Royal Highness,
Jacky, the head honcho,
(more about him later)...

Iris is obsessed with
bath water –
the warmer the better.

She drives the
humans to
distraction with her
purring, paw-dipping
and howls
for a hot drink...

She's also got this thing for the humans
when they're watching movies on the DVD.

She gets all excited
as if they invited her
to join them.

She jumps in their faces
with her sloppy,
            wet purr until
    they
        send her packing...

Olive, on the other hand,

is ALWAYS
brown-nosing up to
          the humans.

She goes into gyrations of joy
whenever anyone
walks near her –

– **and even**
wilder fits of rapture
when someone calls out to her....

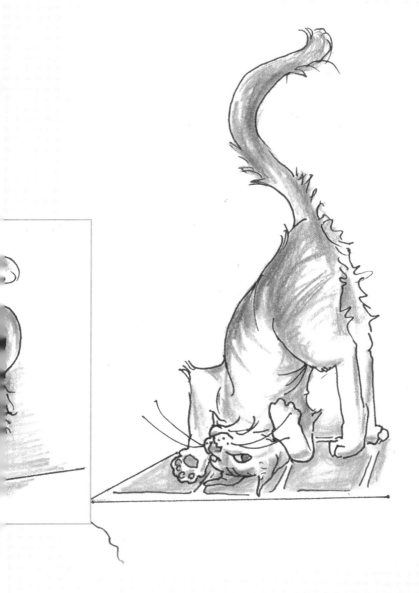

There's a great, big **tangerine tabby**
who lives here, too. He has a wimpy mew,
and has made being lazy a career.

He's called **Pink Cat** because –

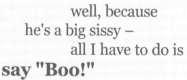

well, because
he's a big sissy –
all I have to do is
say "Boo!"
and he's spooked.

...Then...there's
the **crazy demon** known as **Ma Ma**.'
She claims that her ancestors were royalty
in ancient Egypt — you know, where they used to give
dead cats awesome burials —
but her behavior is
anything but motherly or ladylike...

She is sort of pretty —
in a dangerous kind of way,
with that one golden paw
and gold flecks throughout
her shiny coat — but rumor has it
that she's just
a common stray like the rest of us.
She lives mainly in the garage
during the day and comes
in to sleep with the humans
at night,
but make no mistake —
she holds court
wherever she is at the time...

Ma Ma' relishes tormenting
one of the humans' two pet dogs. Oh, did I fail to
mention them?
No dog has any bearing on this story, except
for the fact that she has one of them
completely buffaloed...   She sits just inside
their dog door waiting for
Rupee the Lab
to plow through it,
cheerful and tongue-lolling...
then, she spits and slaps him
furiously...
he bolts like a shot
back out through
the door in sheer terror,

to a corner of the deck, tail between
his legs, to lick the scratches
on his nose...

Soon he'll forget and try again,
only to be rebuffed in the same way.
Sometimes he gets lucky –
or Ma Ma' is just sleeping.
He sneaks in ever so quietly...
only to discover
her perched on top of the
rabbit hutch, lying in wait
to ambush him
as he passes by!

...Ma Maˊ's got a spit
that'll **melt your whiskers**, and she
dishes it out to whoever
might be sorry enough
to be in her path en route to the garage every morning.

That girl is a real caution!

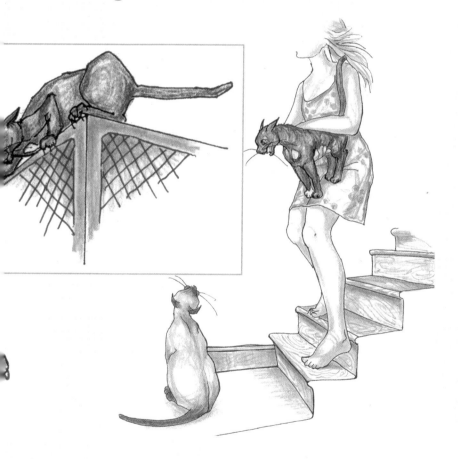

...Here, I can come and go
as I please – as long as
the door's propped open –
and am free to roam the great outdoors –
if I check back in
by dusk.

Every time I venture out in the morning,
I feel a **shiver of anticipation**
rippling up and down my spine.
What thrilling activities
will I enjoy
today?
Off I set, a jungle
panther
stalking other
critters,
big and
small.

But, of course, the most
charmed life is seldom *pur-r-rfect*,
and there's even a downside to living here...

Our tribe is ruled by
a lean, mean, ugly old
bully named **Jacky** with dirty
brown paws, tail and face –
and no matter how much he washes
he doesn't get
any cleaner!

It's a mystery to me why
he thinks HE'S better than the
rest of us. MY paws, by the way,
are ALWAYS snowy,
spotless white.

Whether he discovers me by chance
or shadows me, the outcome is always the same:
he lunges, stops me dead in my tracks...
and **towering and glowering**, dares
me to make one false move.

That's why I retreat ever so carefully –
for the door... because when I try to stand up for myself,
I get into trouble...
Like that unfortunate encounter
with the neighbor cat....

You see,
I'm very sociable
and like making new friends.
This stranger seemed quiet enough
(AND he wasn't very big)...

Being proper on manners, I cautiously
approached him with
a cordial sniff...

He spun
around
in a fury
and chased me
from one end
of our yard
to the other end
of his
and back –

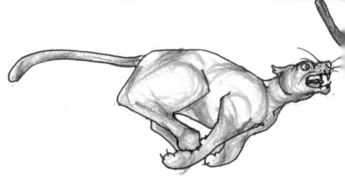

with his razor-sharp fangs
        locked onto my tender
backside! ...Things went
    from bad to worse when
            Doc shaved the base
        of my tail
and everyone laughed
                and called
me **"Poodle"** !

...After all these humiliations,

I returned home.
  I complained
to the smiling cat
          on the wall,
      but he was too
    proud to listen.

      He *did* give me
the time of day, however –
  over and over again,
  even though
  I didn't ask for it...
      I sat there politely
    as he ticked on and on,
        boredom and
        frustration
  building inside me
        by the minute...

Then, out
of the
corner of
one of my
yellow-green
eyes,

I spotted
Olive, that
fussy little
miss who always puts on airs...
She's ***also*** the smallest cat here.
Usually she's painfully alert and poised
to vanish in a heartbeat...

But this time, **I held the advantage** because Mr. Cat-Clock's monotonous conversation (and my handsome resemblance) cloaked my presence...

I sprang...

in a **powerful**
display of
majesty and
menace!

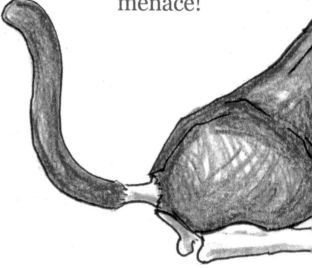

Gleb...the

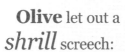

Olive let out a
shrill screech:

"R-a –a –e – e -r-r-r-r-r-r-r-!!!!!!"
She vaulted vertically, and Poof!
disappeared...

Ahhh, that's much better...
Ye all watch out fur-r-r

Terrible!

I love my home. So much so,
      that I can EVEN put up with
the man of the house –

though he doesn't like cats.
         I keep trying to reassure him
that it's all right, I understand,
  and that it's something we could
     probably solve with a few
regular sessions of cat therapy.
  I brush up against his legs,
  chirp-purr to him
      and jump in his lap –
  but I have yet to notice any payoff.

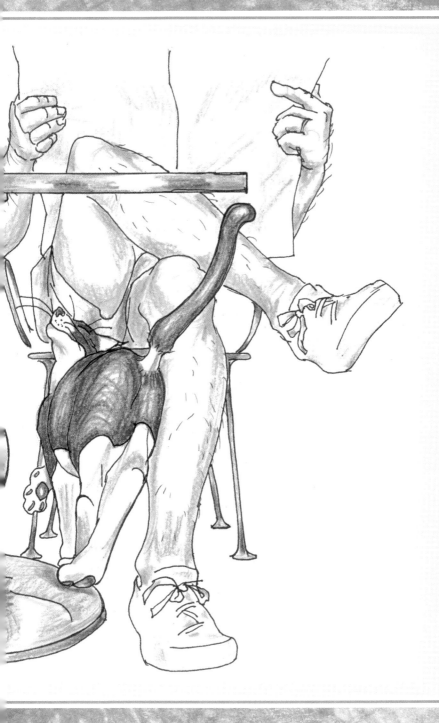

Still – I'm a born optimist, so when I feel discouraged, or just plain worn out from my escapades,

I collapse and . . .

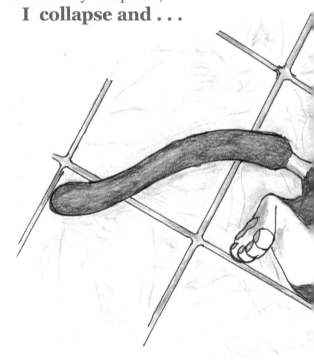

stretch out full length on the kitchen floor –
where I am most underfoot – for a relaxing nap.
Before long, or when somebody trips over me,
I'm fully charged again
and ready to meet what comes.

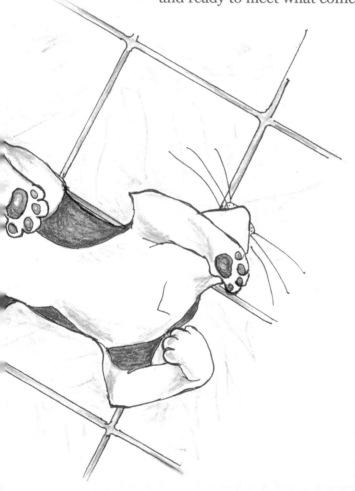

Bring it on, world!

Meanwhile,
I'm waiting
for the fur over my
worry spot

*to grow back – **soon**.*